WORKBOOK

FOR

THE RUTHLESS
ELIMINATION OF
HURRY

(A Guide to John Mark Comer's Book)

The Effective Guide to
Staying Emotionally Healthy
and Spiritually Alive in the
Chaos of the Modern World

HOW TO USE THIS WORKBOOK

- Have a deep and sincere desire to do the things that is recommended here.

- Ponder upon and meditate on the food for thought, reflecting on how they relate to you, what you're advised to do and how to go about doing them.

- In the note section, write down important decisions you've made, relating to the things you've learnt.

- Don't discard this book when you're done with the 7 – Days Program. Instead, always have it in mind, never failing to return when you appear to be deviating.

- Make this a lifestyle. You'd find out that there was far more to gain in the main book through using this practical guide.

- Never assume that the lessons here are difficult and impossible to achieve, they're realistic and made easy for you.

- Follow the daily outline religiously, don't jump days or prioritize one activity over the other.

- Everything outlined here is important for you, don't neglect any.

- We recommend that you spread love and help with this workbook, give people whom you feel would need it. It could go a long way.

ALL THE BEST AS YOU
VENTURE INTO THIS.....

1st DAY

FOOD FOR THOUGHT

It remains very important for you to recognize could be the cause of your stress. After this, you'd accept those out of your control and work on those within your control.

TASK FOR THIS DAY

Find out what has been the cause of your chaos and problems, start creating ways to solve them.

<u>KEEP THIS TO HEART...</u>

Handling the things within your
control impacts positively on the
negative effects of things outside
your control

<u>IMPORTANT
REFLECTIONS (NOTES)</u>

PIN THIS!

Discovering what the problem is remains first step in solving it.

2nd DAY

FOOD FOR THOUGHT

Don't focus your attention and energy on the negative things around you, think about those positive things that make you smile.

TASK FOR THIS DAY

Write down those things and people that make you smile when you remember them. Ponder and feel motivated by it to conquer life.

<u>KEEP THIS TO HEART...</u>

Avoid those toxic things and
people that drain your energy.
Hang around optimistic people.

<u>IMPORTANT</u>
<u>REFLECTIONS (NOTES)</u>

_____

_____

_____

_____

_____

_____

_____

_____

_____

_____

PIN THIS!

You need your energy to conquer
life. No one has the right to drain
you of it.

3rd DAY

FOOD FOR THOUGHT

Concentrate your effort and attention on one thing at a time. Scattered focus increases stress. You could end up chasing the winds when you try everything at once. It is exhausting!

TASK FOR THIS DAY

All your major activities this day should be done one at a time. Stop rushing things.

<u>KEEP THIS TO HEART...</u>

A bird at hand is better that a thousand others in the thick forest.

__IMPORTANT REFLECTIONS (NOTES)__

_____

_____

_____

_____

_____

_____

_____

_____

_____

_____

_____

PIN THIS!

Don't be a jack of all. The most successful people on the planet chose a field and worked on it.

4ᵗʰ DAY

FOOD FOR THOUGHT

Change your routine! That idea of a fixed pattern of activity is very tiring. Try new things, variety is the spice of life.

TASK FOR THIS DAY

Try doing new things this day. Don't continue those old things that drain you. It'd be good to discover new and more efficient strategies that solve your problems.

<u>KEEP THIS TO HEART...</u>

Things get more exhausting
when they keep reoccurring over
and over again.

<u>IMPORTANT</u>
<u>REFLECTIONS (NOTES)</u>

_____

_____

_____

_____

_____

_____

_____

_____

_____

_____

_____

_____

PIN THIS!

Live a flexible life, enjoy it!

5th DAY

FOOD FOR THOUGHT

Accept help from people; hope for the best but expect the worst.

TASK FOR THIS DAY

Realize that you're not omnipotent. Don't set unrealistic goals, also find people to help you.

KEEP THIS TO HEART...

Good friends reduce your
burden, they make life easier.
You won't have to hurry
anymore.

IMPORTANT
REFLECTIONS (NOTES)

_____

_____

_____

_____

_____

_____

_____

_____

_____

_____

_____

_____

_____

_____

_____

_____

_____

_____

_____

_____

_____

_____

_____

_____

_____

PIN THIS!

Surround yourself with people
that make life easier for you.

6th DAY

FOOD FOR THOUGHT

Start taking very good care of yourself. Adequate self-care has its way of making life easier. It reduces stress.

TASK FOR THIS DAY

Find out the things you've been depriving yourself of. As long as they are good for your health, start doing them now.

<u>KEEP THIS TO HEART...</u>

The way you treat yourself is the
prime feeling you get in life. If
the world hates you fine! But it
gets terrible if you hate yourself.

<u>IMPORTANT</u>
<u>REFLECTIONS (NOTES)</u>

_____
_____
_____
_____
_____
_____
_____
_____

_____

PIN THIS!

Always remember that people treat you the way you treat yourself.

7th DAY

FOOD FOR THOUGHT

Clean your space, Freshen up
your environment and freshen up
clutter. This has a cool way
reducing stress and tension.

TASK FOR THIS DAY

Start a cleanup around your
surroundings, free up space and
use some air fresheners. Let cool
scented breeze encompass the
whole place.

KEEP THIS TO HEART...

Your environment has great
impact on your mental health.

IMPORTANT
REFLECTIONS (NOTES)

_____

_____

_____

_____

_____

_____

_____

_____

_____

_____

_____

<u>PIN THIS!</u>

Cleanliness does not cost so
much!

CONGRATULATIONS!

YOU MADE IT TO THE END
OF THE 7 DAYS PROGRAM.

IMBIBE THE THINGS
YOU'VE LEARNT AS A
LIFESTYLE!

Made in the USA
Monee, IL
01 May 2024